NATIONAL
GEOGRAPHIC
KiDS

Funny FiLL-IN

MY HAUNTED HOUSE ADVENTURE

NATIONAL GEOGRAPHIC
WASHINGTON, D.C.

MANNY
FESTATION

How to Play Funny Fill-In!

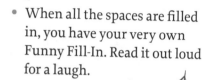

Love to create amazing stories? Good, because this one stars YOU. Get ready to laugh with all your friends—you can play with as many people as you want! Make sure to keep this book on your shelf. You'll want to read it again and again!

Are You Ready to Laugh?

- One person picks a story—you can start at the beginning, the middle, or the end of the book.

- Ask a friend to call out a word that the space asks for—noun, verb, or something else—and write it in the blank space. If there's more than one player, ask the next person to say a word. Extra points for creativity!

- When all the spaces are filled in, you have your very own Funny Fill-In. Read it out loud for a laugh.

- Want to play by yourself? Just fold over the page and use the cardboard insert at the back as a writing pad. Fill in the blank parts of speech list, and copy your answers into the story.

Fun Fact! Make sure you check out the amazing **Fun Facts** that appear on every page!

Parts of Speech

To play the game, you'll need to know how to form sentences. This list with examples of the parts of speech and other terms will help you get started:

Noun: The name of a person, place, thing, or idea
   Examples: tree, mouth, creature
   *The **ocean** is full of colorful **fish**.*

Adjective: A word that describes a noun or pronoun
   Examples: green, lazy, friendly
   *My **silly** dog won't stop laughing!*

Verb: An action word. In the present tense, a verb often ends in –s or –ing. If the space asks for past tense, changing the vowel or adding a –d or –ed to the end usually will set the sentence in the past.
   Examples: swim, hide, plays, running (present tense); biked, rode, jumped (past tense)
   *The giraffe **skips** across the savanna.*
   *The flower **opened** after the rain.*

Adverb: A word that describes a verb and usually ends in –ly
   Examples: quickly, lazily, soundlessly
   *Kelley **greedily** ate all the carrots.*

Plural: More than one
   Examples: mice, telephones, wrenches
   *Why are all the **doors** closing?*

Silly Word or Exclamation: A funny sound, a made-up word, a word you think is totally weird, or a noise someone or something might make
   Examples: Ouch! No way! Foozleduzzle! Yikes!
   *"**Darn!**" shouted Jim. "These cupcakes are sour!"*

Specific Words: There are many more ways to make your story hilarious. When asked for something like a number, animal, or body part, write in something you think is especially funny.

- verb
  - your teacher's name
- type of profession
  - adjective
- number
  - noun
- verb ending in –ing
  - something in a bedroom
- same teacher's name
  - noun
- noun
  - verb
- noun
  - verb ending in –ing
- type of monster, plural
  - celebrity's name
- verb
  - adjective

Fun Fact! One in five Americans believes they've seen or felt a ghost.

Fright Night

It's late when I _____ down the stairs to watch my favorite show, _____:
               verb   *your teacher's name*

Ghost _____ . My mom doesn't like it. She says it gives me _____ nightmares.
         type of profession   *adjective*

But that only happened _____ time(s)—when I thought the ghost of a(n) _____ was
                              number   *noun*

_____ my _____ . Tonight, _____'s team is investigating a
verb ending in –ing   *something in a bedroom*   *same teacher's name*

haunted _____ . Using a spirit _____ , the ghost-hunting team captures the sound of
        noun   *noun*

a voice saying, "_____ here now!" Yikes! I squeeze my stuffed _____ tight. I'm
              verb   *noun*

still _____ when the show ends. Then the star of the show makes an announcement:
     verb ending in–ing

"Friends, we all know that spirits, _____ , and _____ are real. So we're
                          type of monster, plural   *celebrity's name*

having a contest: Anyone with proof that ghosts exist will appear on our next episode." Wow! I need to

make that happen. Time to _____ some _____ ghosts!
                        verb   *adjective*

noun, plural

  something scary

type of toy, plural

  type of liquid

type of pet

  fictional creature

noun

  adjective

type of animal

  noun, plural

noun

  nickname

noun, plural

  silly word

type of gadget

  relative's name

adjective

  verb ending in –ing

noun

Spooktacular Savings

HOLY WATER

EMF

Fun Fact! Ghost hunters use EMF meters that they say work like antennas to check for ghostly disturbances in electromagnetic fields.

Ghostbusting Gadgets

If I'm going to prove that ghosts exist, I need the right _____ . I head to _____ -ville
                                                              noun, plural   *something scary*

Market, where I see voodoo _____ , holy _____ , and lucky _____ feet.
                            type of toy, plural   *type of liquid*   *type of pet*

A lady with hair like a(n) _____ tries to sell me a(n) _____ that she says will make
                            fictional creature   *noun*

me as _____ as a(n) _____ . Luckily, I finally find the _____ that I need
       adjective   *type of animal*   *noun, plural*

under a(n) _____ advertising Spooktacular Savings. But then the lady says, "Be careful, _____ ,
            noun   *nickname*

there are _____ you don't understand." Weird! I try to ask her what she means, but she just loads
            noun, plural

me up with gear: Professor _____ 's EMF Meter and _____ , _____ 's
                            silly word   *type of gadget*   *relative's name*

Extra- _____ Audio Recorder, a copy of *Ghost* _____ *for Kids*, and a(n)
        adjective   *verb ending in –ing*

_____ to wear around my neck for protection. Time to hunt some ghosts!
noun

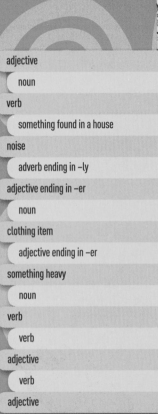

adjective

noun

verb

something found in a house

noise

adverb ending in –ly

adjective ending in –er

noun

clothing item

adjective ending in –er

something heavy

noun

verb

verb

adjective

verb

adjective

Fun Fact! The Bhangarh Fort in India is believed to be so cursed that visitors aren't allowed after dark.

Welcome to Mystery Mansion!

Fortunately, there's a(n) _____ abandoned mansion on _____ Street. Last
                          adjective   noun

Halloween, my friends dared me to _____ on the _____ there. I got to
                     verb   something found in a house

the gate, heard a loud _____ , and ran home _____ . But now I'm feeling
              noise   adverb ending in –ly

a lot _____ , so I grab my gear, a video camera, and a(n) _____ . I put on
    adjective ending in –er   noun

my _____ so I look _____ and head out. Wow, all this stuff weighs
    clothing item   adjective ending in –er

as much as a(n) _____ . So I go back for the wagon I use for my _____ delivery
         something heavy   noun

job. I _____ all the way to the mansion, but _____ when I see a(n) _____ cat at the
   verb   verb   adjective

driveway. We _____ at each other as I walk up to the door. The cat follows me. I try to shoo it
       verb

away—everyone knows black cats are _____ !
                     adjective

verb

verb ending in –ing

adjective

noun, plural

noun

noun

adjective

piece of furniture

same piece of furniture

verb

same verb

body part

verb ending in –s

noun

verb

verb ending in –ing

body part, plural

number

noun, plural

Fun Fact! The White House basement is reportedly haunted by a cat!

Ghostly Greeting

I _____ up to the mansion, the cat _____ after me. The porch is _____ with
   verb   verb ending in –ing   adjective

_____ everywhere. There's a rotting _____ , a black _____ , and a(n) _____
noun, plural   noun   noun   adjective

_____ by the door. As we pass by the _____ , it starts to _____—all
piece of furniture   same piece of furniture   verb

by itself! I'm about to _____ myself, but then the cat rubs up against my _____ and
                   same verb   body part

_____ . Well, if he's not scared, neither am I. I take a deep breath, reach for the _____-shaped
verb ending in –s   noun

knocker, and _____ . Suddenly I hear the sound of _____ _____ coming
            verb   verb ending in –ing   body part, plural

closer, but after waiting for _____ minute(s), no one comes to the door.
                                   number

I yell, "Are there any _____ here?" There's no answer, and when the
                         noun, plural

door finally swings open, there's nobody there!

11

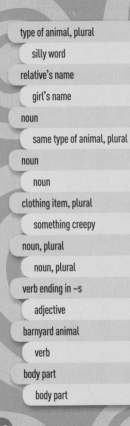

- type of animal, plural
- silly word
- relative's name
- girl's name
- noun
- same type of animal, plural
- noun
- noun
- clothing item, plural
- something creepy
- noun, plural
- noun, plural
- verb ending in –s
- adjective
- barnyard animal
- verb
- body part
- body part

Fun Fact! The first horror movie, called *The Haunted Castle,* was made in 1896. It was only three minutes long!

Ghoul Cat

The inside of the mansion looks just like the house in that movie *Killer Ghost* _____
                                                                              (type of animal, plural)

from Planet _____ . _____ stars as _____ von _____ ,
             (silly word)   (relative's name)   (girl's name)   (noun)

whose house is invaded by ghost _____ , and she saves her _____ using only
                                (same type of animal, plural)   (noun)

a(n) _____ . That movie scared the _____ off me, so I take a minute to look
     (noun)   (clothing item, plural)

around before going in. It's dark, but I can make out _____ , spiderwebs, and _____ .
                                                      (something creepy)   (noun, plural)

I'd rather eat _____ than walk through the door, but the cat _____ into the place
               (noun, plural)   (verb ending in –s)

like he owns it. He's pretty _____ . I don't want him to think I'm a(n) _____ , so
                            (adjective)   (barnyard animal)

I follow him. *Brr!* As I cross the doorway I get a chill. That's when I _____ and see that the cat
                                                                        (verb)

is rubbing his _____ against my _____ . I didn't know cats could be so cold!
               (body part)   (body part)

adjective

    noun

noun

    verb ending in –ed

adjective

    verb ending in –ing

noun, plural

    dance move

your favorite game

    type of instrument

name of a song

    verb

noun, plural

    body part, plural

verb

    same type of instrument

type of animal, plural

Fun Fact! A player piano, or nickelodeon, is a piano that can play all by itself!

We head into a(n) _____ room. There's a crystal _____ hanging from the ceiling and
adjective   noun

peeling wallpaper with a(n) _____ pattern. This must be the room where people _____
noun   verb ending in –ed

long ago. I imagine the _____ parties, the dancing, and _____ that must have
adjective   verb ending in –ing

happened here. I picture ladies wearing fancy _____ on their heads and doing the _____ ,
noun, plural   dance move

while gentlemen played _____ in the corner. I see a(n) _____ and decide
your favorite game   type of instrument

to play _____ . But there's something wrong, because when I go to pick it up, it starts
name of a song

to _____ all by itself! That makes the _____ on my _____ stand up, so I
verb   noun, plural   body part, plural

grab my video camera and _____ instead. Suddenly the cat hisses at the _____
verb   same type of instrument

and tiny _____ scurry out of it. Talk about haunting music!
type of animal, plural

noise

    clothing item

something shiny, plural

    body part

word beginning with *M*

    verb

adjective

    body part, plural

verb

    adjective

noun, plural

    verb ending in –ed

noun

    adjective

your favorite color

    your favorite toy, plural

your favorite movie

    exclamation

body part

Fun Fact! Felidomancy is the belief that the movement of cats can be used to predict the future.

Psyched-Out Psychic

Suddenly there's a(n) _____ (noise) at the door. When I open it, I see a woman wearing a long,

flowing _____ (clothing item) with _____ (something shiny, plural) on her _____ (body part). "My name is

Madam _____ (word beginning with M)," she says. "I _____ (verb) ghosts." She pulls out a(n) _____ (adjective)

ball and tells me to put my _____ (body part, plural) on it. When I do, she says she's getting a message:

"Always _____ (verb) _____ (adjective) _____ (noun, plural), in case you're _____ (verb ending in –ed) by

a(n) _____ (noun)." When I tell her that I don't believe in psychics, she falls into a trance and in

a(n) _____ (adjective) voice says, "You love _____ (your favorite color), _____ (your favorite toy, plural),

and _____ (your favorite movie)." _____ (exclamation)! She's right! Then she says, "There's

a ghost trying to communicate with you right now." But when I look around, there's

just the cat rubbing against my _____ (body part). Silly psychic!

verb

verb

noun

adverb ending in –ly

noun

noun

body part

verb ending in –s

noun

verb

verb ending in –s

verb

noun

verb ending in –ing

verb ending in –ing

adjective

verb

noun

Fun Fact! One of the most famous ghost photographs is of the "Brown Lady" of Raynham Hall, England, descending a flight of stairs.

Halloween Howls

The cat seems to know his way around the house, so I _____ after him. It's too quiet so I start to
verb

_____ . "I was a(n) _____ for Halloween last year," I say to the cat _____ .
verb _noun_ _adverb ending in –ly_

"This year, I'm going to be a(n) _____ . I'm going wear a fake _____ on my _____ ..."
noun _noun_ _body part_

The cat ignores me and _____ up the stairs. That's when I see a flash of white moving at the top.
verb ending in –s

Yikes! I get out my _____ meter and _____ closer. I don't see anything, but something
noun _verb_

_____ my arm! I _____ like a(n) _____ . Then I realize I'm _____
verb ending in –s _verb_ _noun_ _verb ending in –ing_

in front of an open window. And the ghost? It's just a curtain _____ in the wind. I take
verb ending in –ing

a(n) _____ breath and _____ on a nearby _____ . But when I look back at the
adjective _verb_ _noun_

window it's closed. Eerie!

adjective

    noun

noise

    noun

something soft, plural

    verb ending in –s

adverb ending in –ly

    verb ending in –s

verb

    noun, plural

exclamation

    verb

verb ending in –ing

    noun, plural

body part

    noun

Fun Fact! Night-vision devices were first used by soldiers in World War II.

Hoping to pick up some _____ chatter, I turn on my _____ meter. As soon as I do, it starts
                          adjective   noun

to _____ . A(n) _____ must be close by! I look for my video camera and find it under the cat.
      noise   noun

"You're getting _____ all over it!" I cry. The cat _____ _____
                  something soft, plural   verb ending in –s   adverb ending in –ly

but finally _____ off the camera. Great, now the camera won't _____ —the battery must
              verb ending in –s   verb

be dead! I replace the _____ , but now the meter is silent. _____ ! I _____
                          noun, plural   exclamation   verb

around with the meter until it goes off again. I reach for my camera, but the cat is on top of it, _____ .
                                                                                                    verb ending in –ing

And the battery is dead again. What keeps draining all the power? I decide to put my night-vision _____
                                                                                                    noun, plural

on my _____ instead. That's when I notice that the cat is all lit up like
          body part

a holiday _____ !
              noun

verb ending in –ed

verb

adjective

adjective

feeling

verb ending in –ing

adjective

adjective

noun

noun, plural

number

noise

noun

noun, plural

adjective

verb ending in –ing

adjective

Fun Fact! In February 2000, a painting believed to be haunted sold on eBay for more than $1,000!

The cat _____ away and now I can't find him anywhere, so I _____ alone
　　　　　verb ending in –ed　　　　　　　　　　　　　　　　　　　　　　　*verb*

down a(n) _____ and _____ hallway. I'm too _____ to open any
　　　　　　adjective　　　　　*adjective*　　　　　　　*feeling*

of the doors, so I keep going. Suddenly I hear what sounds like _____. But when I look
　　　　　　　　　　　　　　　　　　　　　　　　　　　　　　verb ending in –ing

behind me, there's no one there. Only a(n) _____ painting of a(n) _____ man sitting on
　　　　　　　　　　　　　　　　　　　adjective　　　　　　　　　*adjective*

a(n) _____, holding _____ in his arms. I've taken just _____ more steps
　　　noun　　　　　　　*noun, plural*　　　　　　　　　　　　*number*

when I hear a(n) _____. What was that? I look up at the painting again. But it looks different this
　　　　　　noise

time—there's a(n) _____ where the _____ used to be. How _____. When
　　　　　　　　noun　　　　　　　　*noun, plural*　　　　　　　*adjective*

I look a third time, the man in the painting is _____ with a cat that has
　　　　　　　　　　　　　　　　　　　　verb ending in –ing

_____ eyes and black fur! *Hmm* ... that cat looks very familiar ... Nah, it couldn't be!
　adjective

- noun
  - noun
- verb
  - verb ending in –ing
- adjective
  - verb ending in –s
- color
  - clothing item, plural
- noun
  - clothing item
- verb ending in –ing
  - noun
- adjective
  - verb ending in –s
- type of animal, plural
  - adjective
- body part
  - body part

24

Fun Fact! King Tut was buried with clothes suited for almost any afterlife occasion—including 145 loincloths!

Up ahead there's a(n) _____ (noun) leading to the attic. What a great place to find a spooky _____ (noun)!

I climb up, but I _____ (verb) when I hear a sound. Something's _____ (verb ending in –ing) around up here. Lots of somethings! A(n) _____ (adjective) shape _____ (verb ending in –s) by overhead, wearing a(n) _____ (color) nighty. A pair of upside-down _____ (clothing item, plural) are climbing up the _____ (noun). An old _____ (clothing item) is _____ (verb ending in –ing) right at me! It smacks into a(n) _____ (noun) and a(n) _____ (adjective) creature _____ (verb ending in –s) out. These aren't ghosts at all, they're only _____ (type of animal, plural)!

So I decide to join in the fun. I put an old _____ (adjective) hat on my _____ (body part). Then I find some socks and put them on my _____ (body part). The cat gives me a round of ap-paws and we decide to move on.

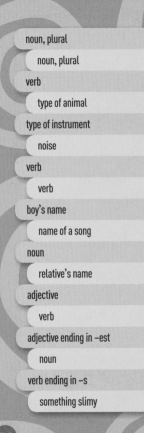

- noun, plural
- noun, plural
- verb
- type of animal
- type of instrument
- noise
- verb
- verb
- boy's name
- name of a song
- noun
- relative's name
- adjective
- verb
- adjective ending in –est
- noun
- verb ending in –s
- something slimy

Fun Fact! The Musical Jolly Chimp toy originated in Japan in the 1950s and has appeared in scary books, movies, and TV shows ever since.

I find the cat in the nursery, where the walls are lined with _____ and stacks of
                                                                 noun, plural

_____ are on the floor. Wow, these kids must have really liked to _____ .
noun, plural   verb

I see a toy _____ holding a(n) _____ . But when I turn my back I
              type of animal   type of instrument

suddenly hear a(n) _____ ! I _____ back around. Did that toy just _____ on its
                     noise   verb   verb

own? I wind up a(n) _____-in-the-Box, and it plays " _____ " and out pops
                      boy's name   name of a song

a creepy _____ . I jump, but when I land I must have stepped on a doll, because it starts to say
           noun

" _____ " over and over again. Enough of this _____ nursery. I start to _____
    relative's name   adjective   verb

out of the room, but I trip over the _____ thing yet—a stuffed _____ . It _____
                                       adjective ending in –est   noun   verb ending in –s

at me, covering me in _____ ! Yuck!
                        something slimy

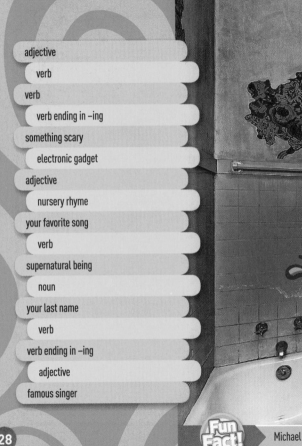

- adjective
  - verb
- verb
  - verb ending in –ing
- something scary
  - electronic gadget
- adjective
  - nursery rhyme
- your favorite song
  - verb
- supernatural being
  - noun
- your last name
  - verb
- verb ending in –ing
  - adjective
- famous singer

Fun Fact! Michael Jackson's video for "Thriller" is the only music video to be added to America's National Film Registry.

Boo-gie Nights

I've just had a(n) _____ idea. If I can't find a ghost, maybe I can get one to _____ to me!
adjective _verb_

I get out my camera and _____ around, trying to take pictures with it. But something isn't
verb

right. Then I remember reading on _____ _____.*com* that some ghosts are
verb ending in –ing _something scary_

attracted to old music. I pull out my _____—darn, I only have _____ songs.
electronic gadget _adjective_

So instead I start to sing " _____ " and " _____ ." Then I
nursery rhyme _your favorite song_

try " _____ like a(n) _____ " by DJ _____ _____ . Suddenly
verb _supernatural being_ _noun_ _your last name_

the cat appears. Where did he _____ from? And is he _____ to my song?
verb _verb ending in –ing_

I take a ton of pictures—I may not find a real ghost, but I bet " _____ cat" will
adjective

be an Internet hit! He has better moves than _____ !
famous singer

kitchen appliance

    adjective

noun

    type of food

something round, plural

    type of animal

noun, plural

    adjective

verb

    noun, plural

noun

    noun, plural

noun

    verb

your age

    verb

body part

FLOUR

Fun Fact! The shiny coating on some candies, such as jelly beans, is made from the excretion of the Kerria lacca bug.

Ghostly Prints

I head for the kitchen. Maybe the _____ (kitchen appliance) is haunted. Also, I'm _____ (adjective) and need

a(n) _____ (noun). I open the cupboards and find _____ (type of food) chowder, spaghetti and

_____ (something round, plural), and _____ (type of animal) noodle soup. Then I spot a jar marked _____ (noun, plural),

but when I open the lid there's only flour inside. That's when I get a(n) _____ (adjective) idea about how to

prove ghosts exist. I _____ (verb) around the kitchen, spreading flour all over the _____ (noun, plural),

the _____ (noun), and the floor. If there's a ghost here, it'll leave its _____ (noun, plural) in the flour! Then

I hide behind a large _____ (noun) in the corner and _____ (verb). After _____ (your age) minutes

I hear something and _____ (verb) out with my camera ready. There are _____ (body part)-prints all

over the place and they lead to ... the cat!

FLOUR

- verb
- adjective
- something tall, plural
- something round
- verb
- friend's name
- verb ending in –s
- noun, plural
- noise
- verb
- noun
- feeling
- verb
- noun
- body part
- something heavy, plural
- adjective
- type of animal
- type of insect

Fun Fact! Fireflies aren't flies, they're beetles. In some species, even the eggs and larvae glow.

Seeing Stars

Next, I _____ outside. The backyard is full of _____ _____ .
verb adjective something tall, plural

A(n) _____ swing hangs from one, so I _____ on it. I look up at the stars and see the
something round verb

_____ constellation. Suddenly a star leaves the sky and _____ toward me! An orb!
friend's name verb ending in –s

Ghost hunters love _____ ! I start taking pictures, but I hear an eerie _____ above
noun, plural noise

me and _____ my _____ . Oh no! I've made the spirits _____ ! I start
verb noun feeling

to _____ but don't see the _____ in front of me. I step on it, and it flies up and hits me on
verb noun

the _____ ! I drop like a sack of _____ . When I come to, I see _____
body part something heavy, plural adjective

eyes blinking above me. A(n) _____ ! It must have made the scary noise I heard. Then the orb
type of animal

lands on me and I realize it's just a fire-_____ .
type of insect

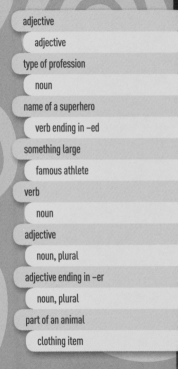

- adjective
  - adjective
- type of profession
  - noun
- name of a superhero
  - verb ending in –ed
- something large
  - famous athlete
- verb
  - noun
- adjective
  - noun, plural
- adjective ending in –er
  - noun, plural
- part of an animal
  - clothing item

Fun Fact! At Greyfriars Kirkyard, a Scottish graveyard, there's a monument to Greyfriars Bobby, a dog who refused to leave its owner's grave.

Tombstone Ticklers

I see something _____ by the fence and decide to inspect it. Jackpot! A graveyard. There has to
                  adjective

be a ghost here! I don't know who used to live here, but these tombstones are _____ . They say things
                                                                              adjective

like "World-famous _____ and _____ -lover" and "RIP _____ :
                    type of profession   noun   name of a superhero

We'll always remember the day you _____ the _____ ." But my favorite has
                                   verb ending in –ed   something large

to be "Here lies _____ , who discovered the true meaning of life: _____ for
                 famous athlete   verb

the _____ , and don't take any _____ _____ ." Off to the side, I see
    noun   adjective   noun, plural

a(n) _____ tombstone. There's _____ covering it, so I can
     adjective ending in –er   noun, plural

only make out "you had the softest _____ ." They must have buried
                                    part of an animal

their pets here, too! Out of nowhere, the cat jumps out at me and I nearly leap

out of my _____ !
           clothing item

MANNY FESTATION

35

adjective

verb

noun, plural

noun

verb ending in –ing

noun

noun

body part, plural

verb ending in –ing

verb

noun

adverb ending in –ly

feeling

nickname

adjective

same nickname

Fun Fact! Séances grew popular during the Civil War because people wanted to communicate with their dead fathers and sons.

The Scare-Taker

I'm happy I've found the cat again—ghost hunting isn't for the _____ at heart. As we _____
                                                                    adjective   verb

through the yard, _____ cover the moon, making it look as dark out as a(n) _____ .
                          noun, plural   noun

In the shadows I see something _____ right at us! It looks like a ghost carrying
                                        verb ending in –ing

a(n) _____ and wearing a(n) _____ on its head. Eek! I'm so scared my _____
          noun   noun   body part, plural

are _____ , but I get out my camera anyway. I _____ closer and press
        verb ending in –ing   verb

the button. But when the flash goes off, I see it's just a caretaker carrying a big _____ .
                                                                                                    noun

He looks at us _____ and says, "I'm so _____ you've found
                    adverb ending in –ly   feeling

someone to take care of you, _____ !" He must be _____ . Who
                                    nickname   adjective

is _____ , anyway?
      same nickname

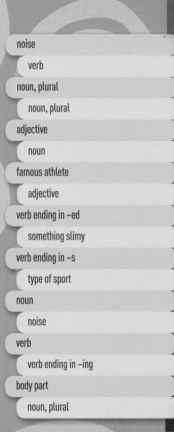

- noise
  - verb
- noun, plural
  - noun, plural
- adjective
  - noun
- famous athlete
  - adjective
- verb ending in –ed
  - something slimy
- verb ending in –s
  - type of sport
- noun
  - noise
- verb
  - verb ending in –ing
- body part
  - noun, plural

Fun Fact! In the 1800s, "body snatchers" robbed bodies from graves and sold them to medical schools to use to train new doctors.

Barely Bones

_____! What was that? I _____ across the lawn, trampling _____ and
   noise   verb   noun, plural

leaping over prickly _____ . As I get closer to a shed, I hear a long _____ moan.
                                noun, plural   adjective

_____ at the ready, I kick in the door like _____ and shine my _____ light
   noun   famous athlete   adjective

around. Suddenly I'm _____ to the ground, and _____ _____ itself
                           verb ending in −ed   something slimy   verb ending in −s

around me. I do my best _____ move and it falls off me. Then I realize it was just a garden
                                 type of sport

hose. It must have fallen off the _____ . Oops. Just then there's a(n) _____ at the
                                   noun   noise

window. I turn ... and see a skeleton! I _____ in terror. The skeleton's _____ at
                                       verb   verb ending in −ing

me! Its _____ is the most terrifying thing I've ever seen. I feel around for
           body part

my flashlight and turn it on. Oh, come on! It's just a tree branch that has lost

all its _____ !
     noun, plural

- verb
  - adjective
- verb
  - type of animal
- body part
  - body part
- adjective
  - noun
- verb
  - adjective
- type of profession
  - verb
- verb ending in –ing
  - adjective

Fun Fact! Some ancient Egyptians mummified their pets. They even mummified fish, crocodiles, and beetles.

M-M-Mummy?

I _____ onto a(n) _____ bench and sit down to _____. How will I ever find a ghost
verb _adjective_ _verb_

now? I suddenly feel _____-webs brush against my _____. When I try to
type of animal _body part_

brush them off, my_____ gets tangled in them. These are some _____ webs! I try
body part _adjective_

to tear them using my _____, but that just makes me _____ even more. That's when
noun _verb_

I realize that these aren't webs at all, they're _____ bandages. And the bench? It's a crypt! I'm
adjective

no _____, but I know a mummy when I feel one! I try to _____ away, but I'm
type of profession _verb_

trapped. I roll on the ground, _____ the whole time. That's when I see they aren't bandages
verb ending in –ing

at all, they're _____ paper that someone had wound around the trees. How did I get
adjective

wrapped up in all this anyway?

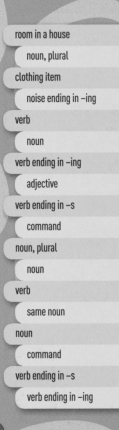

- room in a house
  - noun, plural
- clothing item
  - noise ending in –ing
- verb
  - noun
- verb ending in –ing
  - adjective
- verb ending in –s
  - command
- noun, plural
  - noun
- verb
  - same noun
- noun
  - command
- verb ending in –s
  - verb ending in –ing

Fun Fact! Traditionally, a divining rod is a forked tree branch used to detect things buried underground.

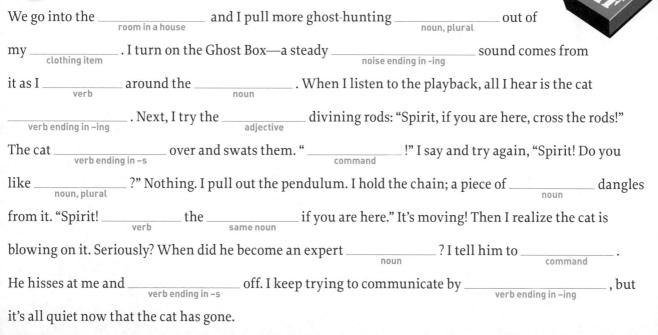

We go into the _____ and I pull more ghost-hunting _____ out of
          room in a house   noun, plural

my _____ . I turn on the Ghost Box—a steady _____ sound comes from
   clothing item   noise ending in -ing

it as I _____ around the _____ . When I listen to the playback, all I hear is the cat
      verb   noun

_____ . Next, I try the _____ divining rods: "Spirit, if you are here, cross the rods!"
verb ending in –ing   adjective

The cat _____ over and swats them. " _____ !" I say and try again, "Spirit! Do you
     verb ending in –s   command

like _____ ?" Nothing. I pull out the pendulum. I hold the chain; a piece of _____ dangles
   noun, plural   noun

from it. "Spirit! _____ the _____ if you are here." It's moving! Then I realize the cat is
        verb   same noun

blowing on it. Seriously? When did he become an expert _____ ? I tell him to _____ .
                                     noun   command

He hisses at me and _____ off. I keep trying to communicate by _____ , but
            verb ending in –s   verb ending in –ing

it's all quiet now that the cat has gone.

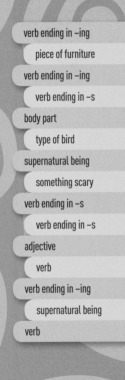

- verb ending in –ing
  - piece of furniture
- verb ending in –ing
  - verb ending in –s
- body part
  - type of bird
- supernatural being
  - something scary
- verb ending in –s
  - verb ending in –s
- adjective
  - verb
- verb ending in –ing
  - supernatural being
- verb

Fun Fact! When the Marshmallow Man exploded in the movie *Ghostbusters*, special effects crews used shaving cream to cover the actors.

Ghost-Busted

The sun is _____ up when I find the cat hiding under a(n) _____ .
                verb ending in –ing   piece of furniture

I tell him I'm sorry for _____ . He purrs and _____ up against
                        verb ending in –ing   verb ending in –s

my _____ . Ghostbusting might have been a bust, but at least I made a new friend. I
    body part

decide to cheer us up by telling a joke: "What do you get when you cross a(n) _____ with
                                                                              type of bird

a(n) _____ ? A(n) _____ that _____ !" The cat just _____ .
     supernatural being   something scary   verb ending in –s   verb ending in –s

What a(n) _____ cat! It's time for me to leave. I walk outside then _____ , but the cat's gone.
          adjective   verb

I look up and see him _____ in the attic window. How did he get up there so fast? Maybe
                      verb ending in –ing

he saw a(n) _____ ! I'm tempted to go back, but my parents will be up soon.
            supernatural being

I'd better _____ .
           verb

adjective

    verb ending in –ing

verb ending in –ing

    something bright

adjective

    type of profession, plural

verb

    exotic location

adjective

    noun, plural

clothing item

    piece of furniture

body part

    verb

verb ending in –s

    adjective

Fun Fact! Stargate was a real United States government program that studied paranormal phenomena.

At home, I check the pictures I took—just a(n) _____ shape in the background could win me the
adjective

contest! Oh man, the cat is _____ in every picture! Then I notice something odd. I can see
verb ending in –ing

right through him—and he's _____ like a(n) _____ ! The cat is a ghost! I'm
verb ending in –ing   _something bright_

so excited, until I realize I can't tell anyone. His home would be invaded by_____ ghost hunters,
adjective

_____ wanting to _____ him, and agents from _____ offering him
type of profession, plural   _verb_   _exotic location_

_____ _____ . So instead I decide to hang up my ghost-hunting _____ once
adjective   _noun, plural_   _clothing item_

and for all. I go to the living room and flop onto a(n) _____ and turn on the TV. _On the Trail_
piece of furniture

_of Big-_____ is just finishing up, and the host says: "_____ up,
body part   _verb_

viewers at home: If you want to be on the show, all you have to do is find proof that

the creature _____ ." What a(n) _____ idea!
verb ending in –s   _adjective_

47

Credits

Cover, 3D JML/iStock; 4, Albund/Shutterstock; 6, Anneka/Shutterstock; 8, Vinterriket/Shutterstock; 10, Anastasios Kandris/Shutterstock; 12, Stanislav Bokach/Shutterstock; 14, Elpis Ioannidis/Shutterstock; 16, Jeff Dalton/Shutterstock; 18, Olena Rublenko/Shutterstock; 20, Photogl/Shutterstock; 22, badahos/Shutterstock; 24, Yu Lan/Shutterstock; 26, Haveseen/Shutterstock; 28, Pics721/Shutterstock; 30, Anders Photo/Shutterstock; 32, Zoltan Fabian/iStock; 34, Hollygraphic/Shutterstock; 36, fotozambra/iStock; 38, LoloStock/Shutterstock; 40, E. Sweet/Shutterstock; 42, Iriana Shiyan/Shutterstock; 44, Vinterriket/Shutterstock; 46, AnnalA/Shutterstock

Published by the National Geographic Society

Staff for This Book

Ariane Szu-Tu, *Project Editor*
James Hiscott, Jr., and Callie Broaddus, *Art Directors*
Kelley Miller, *Senior Photo Editor*
Jennifer MacKinnon, *Writer*
Kevin Rechin, *Illustrator*
Paige Towler, *Editorial Assistant*
Rachel Kenny and Sanjida Rashid, *Design Production Assistants*
Michael Cassady and Colm McKeveny, *Rights Clearance Specialists*
Grace Hill, *Managing Editor*
Mike O'Connor, *Production Editor*
Lewis R. Bassford, *Production Manager*
Jenn Hoff, *Manager, Production Services*
Susan Borke, *Legal and Business Affairs*

Published by the National Geographic Society

Gary E. Knell, *President and CEO*
John M. Fahey, *Chairman of the Board*
Melina Gerosa Bellows, *Chief Education Officer*
Declan Moore, *Chief Media Officer*
Hector Sierra, *Senior Vice President and General Manager, Book Division*

Senior Management Team, Kids Publishing and Media

Nancy Laties Feresten, *Senior Vice President*
Jennifer Emmett, *Vice President, Editorial Director, Kids Books*
Julie Vosburgh Agnone, *Vice President, Editorial Operations*
Rachel Buchholz, *Editor and Vice President*, NG Kids *magazine*
Michelle Sullivan, *Vice President, Kids Digital*
Eva Absher-Schantz, *Design Director*
Jay Sumner, *Photo Director*
Hannah August, *Marketing Director*
R. Gary Colbert, *Production Director*

Digital

Anne McCormack, *Director*
Laura Goertzel, Sara Zeglin, *Producers*
Emma Rigney, *Creative Producer*
Bianca Bowman, *Assistant Producer*
Natalie Jones, *Senior Product Manager*

Editorial, Design, and Production by Plan B Book Packagers

The National Geographic Society is one of the world's largest nonprofit scientific and educational organizations. Founded in 1888 to "increase and diffuse geographic knowledge," the Society's mission is to inspire people to care about the planet. It reaches more than 400 million people worldwide each month through its official journal, *National Geographic*, and other magazines; National Geographic Channel; television documentaries; music; radio; films; books; DVDs; maps; exhibitions; live events; school publishing programs; interactive media; and merchandise. National Geographic has funded more than 10,000 scientific research, conservation, and exploration projects and supports an education program promoting geographic literacy.

For more information, please visit nationalgeographic.com, call 1-800-NGS LINE (647-5463), or write to the following address:

National Geographic Society, 1145 17th Street N.W., Washington, D.C. 20036-4688 U.S.A.

Visit us online at nationalgeographic.com/books

For librarians and teachers: ngchildrensbooks.org

More for kids from National Geographic: kids.nationalgeographic.com

For information about special discounts for bulk purchases, please contact National Geographic Books Special Sales: ngspecsales@ngs.org

For rights or permissions inquiries, please contact National Geographic Books Subsidiary Rights: ngbookrights@ngs.org

ISBN: 978-1-4263-2064-4
Printed in China

15/RRDS/1